HOW TO BUILD A
SIX-FIGURE
BUSINESS
WHILE WORKING A 9 TO 5

A Practical Guide to Running a Successful
Business While Working Full-Time

Kimmoly LaBoo

For information regarding special discounts for bulk purchases, please contact the publisher: LaBoo Publishing Enterprise, LLC

staff@laboopublishing.com
www.laboopublishing.com

Printed in the United States of America

TABLE OF CONTENTS

INTRODUCTION

Welcome to *How to Build a Six-Figure Business While Working a 9-to-5: A Practical Guide to Running a Successful Business While Working Full-Time.*

You picked up this book because you're ready to step out of the ordinary. You've dreamed of financial freedom, pursuing your passions, and creating a better future—all while managing the demands of a full-time job. While the idea of building a business alongside your 9-to-5 may feel overwhelming, it's more achievable than you think.

Many of the world's most successful businesses began as side hustles, nurtured in spare moments. This book is your step-by-step guide to making it happen, filled with practical strategies, personal insights, and inspiration from my own journey of growing a six-figure business while working full-time.

I've been where you are—balancing work deadlines, family responsibilities, and big dreams with limited time and resources. This isn't about quick fixes or lofty promises. It's about sustainable growth, smart time management, and leveraging your current job as a foundation to build something extraordinary.

If you've ever felt like there aren't enough hours in the day, struggled with financial constraints, or doubted your ability to succeed, this guide will show you how to turn those challenges into opportunities. You'll learn how to optimize your time, market your business on a budget, and create systems that allow your business to grow—even when you're not actively working on it.

This book is for the dreamers and doers, the visionaries ready to turn their side hustle into a six-figure reality without sacrificing stability or security. The journey isn't easy, but it's worth it. Let's start building the life you deserve.

To your success,
Kimmoly

CHAPTER 1
Break Free:
Overcome The 9-to-5 Grind

As an entrenched part of modern life, the 9-to-5 routine has brought some of us decades of stability and a steady paycheck. For others, it brings solace and certainty. It is, for many, a straitjacket that constrains creativity, personal autonomy, and growth potential. Breaking free from this grind doesn't involve quitting your job on a whim. Instead, it's about changing your mindset and setting yourself up for financial freedom through starting a business.

Escape is not a call to abandon and critique the value of your job but to realize it's a launchpad. By redefining your career, you can build the life you want around your job.

The mind shift: Think beyond the job

Making the leap out of the 9-to-5 paradigm starts with a simple change in perspective. Many of us are raised with the idea that traditional work is the safest, most stable route to a secure future.

We are taught to choose predictability over risk and a steady paycheck over our personal dreams. Although these beliefs offer reassurance, they usually exact a price from us by suppressing our greatness.

To break free of a 9-to-5 and begin crafting something bigger, you have to adopt a new mindset. You must have a growth mindset, one demanding you to take on challenges, to appreciate learning through your life, and to believe that you can succeed. Identification with a growth mindset enables one to see roadblocks not as impassable walls but as opportunities to develop, adapt and flourish.

Creating the Mind Shift Questions

A shift in mindset isn't a flip of a switch—it begins with asking yourself thought-provoking questions that profoundly challenge the status quo and, ultimately, help you create clarity around what you truly want.

Reflect on the following:

What is my definition of financial freedom?

What does having financial freedom mean to me?

Everyone envisions financial freedom differently. For some it could be the freedom to travel, the ability to live without debt. For others, it may involve supporting their family or having the freedom to try out passion projects. Being clear on your version of financial freedom is important because it introduces order to your adventure of entrepreneurship.

What would my life look like if I generated my own income streams?

Think of the potential for freedom if you weren't tied to that first paycheck anymore. What doors would open? What would you do with your time? As an entrepreneur, you may have more flexible working hours compared to a regular job.

How far will I go to make this happen?

When you're starting a business, it takes sacrifice. Consider what you're willing to sacrifice in the short term — be it less leisure time, earlier wake-ups or weekends devoted to your business. Being honest about your willingness to sacrifice is a key element of your mindset shift.

Changing the Way You Think About Your Job

If you have a job, instead of looking at it as a hindrance, start looking at it as a resource, a means to get what you want. When I did this, everything shifted for me.

Your 9-to-5 provides a number of advantages that can help you build your business:

- **Financial Stability:** Your paycheck means you can invest in your business without the immediate pressure of having to monetize it.

- **Skill Development**: Skills that you use at work, like communication, organization or problem solving, can directly help your entrepreneurial efforts.

- **A Safety Net**: Your job gives you stability so you can take calculated risks without compromising your basic needs.

Recast your job as a vehicle rather than a destination; your job is a means to an end.

Transitioning from Employee Mindset to an Entrepreneur Mindset

Thinking beyond your job is seeing yourself as more than an employee. It's seeing yourself as someone who has the power to forge your own opportunities. This step will help frame the challenges you face as paving stones, the foundation for what lies ahead and the success you will achieve.

This is the transformation of mindset, which is the first step from vision to reality. Your journey starts here.

Conceptualizing Financial Freedom as an Act of Entrepreneurship

Financial independence is being able to definitely pay for life in your own way without depending only on a 9-to-5 paycheck. One of the most powerful routes to that freedom is through entrepreneurship. When you have a 9-to-5 job, your earning potential is mostly limited by the salary structures — but when you run your own business, you dictate your income. Your business success is completely based on the effort you put forth in your business.

Entrepreneurship is not about jumping head-first into the pool with no preparation. It's about beginning small, experimenting with your ideas and developing your confidence incrementally. Building your business while employed lowers the risk of financial loss and sets the stage for growth.

Finding What You Are Good At and Enjoy

The first step toward freedom from the 9-to-5 is recognizing what you already have available to share. Most people think they need a game-changing idea in order to start a business when in fact, the truth is the exact opposite. Most successful businesses are based on simple ideas executed to perfection. Only you can draw upon a unique combination of skills, hobbies, and past experiences to create the basis for a profitable side gig.

All it entails is providing value to the world based on your strengths. It involves critically assessing your strengths and passions.

Assess Your Skills

Your talents are the foundation of your future company. Begin by considering what comes to you naturally and the skills you've developed over the years. These don't have to be extraordinary or groundbreaking — many successful entrepreneurs have created businesses based on everyday skills.

Ask yourself:

- **What do I excel at?** Consider the tasks that come easily to you — perhaps technical skills like graphic design, writing, or coding, or soft skills like communication, organization, or leadership.

People tell me I'm a great listener and that I'm compassionate. These things show up in my business daily. Others' feedback can illuminate strengths you may not give yourself credit for.

- **What have I learned — at work or in life?** Skills you've learned in jobs, hobbies or volunteer work — like budgeting, project management or event planning — can be great assets when building a business.

Start a list of your talents, even the smallest ones. These are the skills that you can begin with. Take a moment to write a few here.

_____   _____

_____   _____

_____   _____

Explore Your Passions

We can always learn the skills needed, but passion keeps you motivated in the face of obstacles. When starting a business based on something you give a darn about, you are likely to succeed because you will have fun doing it, and you will fight through the difficult moments.

Here's how to discover your passions:

What brings you joy? Think about things that interest you and that make time fly.

What do you care deeply about? What hobby or lifestyle personally speaks to you?

What would you do if you weren't paid? The response to this question usually leads to something you truly like doing.

If you are passionate about helping people to transform their lives, for instance, you could look into coaching or consulting. If you have a creative passion, perhaps you can open a business in the world of art, writing or crafting. The trick is to match your passions to practical opportunities.

Identify Market Needs

Your skills and passion won't be enough: Your market gap is a critical factor in business success. Consider what problems you can solve or what gaps in the market you may be able to fill. Consider questions like:

What problems do people have that I can solve for them?

What products or services do I wish were available?

What special gifts do I bring to fulfill them?

Ultimately, you need to reach the intersection of your skills, talents, passions, and what people will pay for.

Steps You Can Take to Start Finding Income Streams

- **Skills and Interest List:** List everything you enjoy, excel in, and have experience with. Write it all down—don't be shy.

- **Research Options:** Find products or services that could be a new use for your skills and interests. If you have a passion for photography, you can start offering professional headshots or selling stock images.

- **Validate:** Identify a small product or service that you can start with. Try it with friends and family or a small group and get constructive feedback to help refine your approach.

- **Seek Advice:** Test your ideas out with trusted friends or family who can give you constructive feedback. Gathering information from online communities and forums can also provide constructive input.

- **Learn From the Success of Others:** Research your competitors. Figure out what they do right and how you might put a fresh spin on the market.

Learning about someone else's success can inspire and motivate you to take that leap. These are just a few examples of people who started small and built their companies over time.

The Weekend Freelancer: A marketing professional used weekends to provide freelance social media services. They gradually grew a client base and ended up firing their agency and going full time running their own agency.

The Hobby Entrepreneur: A teacher with a love of baking decided to sell cupcakes at local markets. What started as a side hustle quickly turned into a booming bakery.

The Skill Monetizer: An I.T. professional started offering coding lessons via online courses in his free time. The courses took off and he set up a steady passive income stream.

These stories show that you don't have to make radical change overnight. Slow progress with systematic approach leads to long-term victory.

Relaxing Your Mind and Gaining Confidence

Fear is the most common obstacle to taking the first step toward entrepreneurship. Whether it's the fear of failure, or success, judgment or the unknown, these feelings are normal but can be dealt with.

Here's how to tackle them:

- **Do Not Eat the Whole Elephant:** Break the process into small, actionable steps that will reinforce your sense of accomplishment. Every little victory continues to build your confidence.

- **Educate Yourself:** Lack of knowledge increases uncertainty. Get to know as much as possible about your business idea, the market, and ways you can work around it.

- **Launch, Launch, Launch—Why wait for perfection:** It's better to launch an imperfect product or service than wait for the ideal moment. It's more important to make progress — not perfection.

- **Build a Support System:** Be around people who are on the same path as you and can support your goals. Friends, family, or online communities — having support helps.

When I started my business, I didn't have it all figured out—far from it. What I did have was a deep desire to help others bring their stories to life through writing and publishing. I wanted to create a space where they could pour their creativity, pain, joy, and experiences onto the page.

With years of writing experience and several published titles under my belt, I had built a foundation of knowledge. But when God placed this vision on my heart, I didn't hesitate. I didn't overthink, second-guess, or give doubt a chance to creep in. Instead, I put a plan in motion and took action. I trusted myself, knowing that anything I didn't yet know, I could learn along the way.

I started, and I never stopped. If I had waited for the perfect moment, hundreds of authors might still be searching for a way to share their brilliant ideas with the world. Instead, I get to witness their dreams become reality—one book at a time. My imperfect beginning has blossomed into something beautiful, not just for me, but for every incredible author I've had the privilege to work with. And for that, I am deeply grateful.

Design a Vision for Your Future

Having a vision gives you focus and motivation on harder days. Take time to define:

> **Your Goals**: What do you want to accomplish over the next year, the next five years, and beyond? Establish concrete, quantifiable goals.

> **Your Why:** What does being financially independent mean to you? Does your "why" propel your motivation?

> **Your Plan:** Start with your vision and break it down into actionable steps. A well-defined plan transforms dreams to reality.

8 Hacks to Manage Your Time as an Entrepreneur

Managing a full-time job and a growing business is finessing time management. Here are practical tips to get things done:

> **Focus:** On tasks that make the biggest difference in your business.

> **Productivity Tools:** Use apps such as Trello, Asana and even Google Calendar for organizing and tracking your tasks.

Set Boundaries: Allocate dedicated time blocks to your business, and guard them from distractions.

Get Rid of Non-Value Adding Waste: Identify activities that don't add value and minimize or remove these actions.

Take the First Step

The first (and most significant) step to escaping the 9-to-5 grind is actually one small step. Whether it is writing down your business idea, researching your market, creating a simple product, **the important part is to get started**. Each step forward has a compounding effect towards your goals.

You don't have to leave your job to begin. Use it as a springboard to realize your dreams and build a base. Financial freedom is feasible, and every step you take today lays the foundation for a better tomorrow.

CHAPTER 2
Bet on Yourself: Work Harder for You Than You Do for Them

Success starts with what you believe. You must believe in YOU, believe in what you are capable of achieving and what you envision for yourself. As an employee in a 9-to-5 position, it's easy to devote all your attention to advancing someone else's ideas while forgoing your own ambition. However, the path to a successful business requires a change of mindset. You need to make yourself a priority, and you need to make a commitment to build a future that matches your dreams and goals. This chapter will have you betting on yourself, developing unbreakable confidence, and seizing every opportunity to inch yourself closer to your dreams.

The Power of Self-Confidence

Self-confidence is the cornerstone of success. It's not merely a transient experience — it's a skill you can practice and build over time. Self-confidence gives you the courage to take risks and make decisions and combat questions about your resilience. Without it, you may doubt your capabilities and keep yourself from achieving greatness. The good news is self-confidence is not something you're either born with or without; it's a mindset and practice that anyone can cultivate.

You cannot bet on yourself if you don't believe in yourself first. We're all skilled, experienced, and have qualities that are unique and valuable. The energy you spend creating someone else's dream in your 9-to-5 can also be harnessed toward your own dream. However, this shift in focus opens new doors to personal and financial opportunities and strengthens your belief in your own abilities.

How Confidence Grows

Self-confidence is not something that happens overnight. It's a cycle of doing, reflecting and being open to learning. Here are three critical approaches for developing and maintaining your confidence:

> ➤ **Act Regardless of Confusion**
> Taking action — even if the outcome is uncertain — is one of the best things you can do to nurture confidence. Waiting for the "perfect moment" or hoping to have all the answers at the outset can lead to paralysis. Instead, set small, achievable goals to work toward. Every little action you take builds momentum and affirms that you are capable of real progress.
>
> If you're launching a business, for example, begin with a basic plan, or approach prospective customers and

see what happens. With experience and results, your self-trust will grow, naturally. The solution is to just accept the uncertainty and realize that the real learning actually occurs on the journey.

➢ **Acknowledge Your Strengths**
Identifying and celebrating your strengths is another important component of self-confidence. Too many individuals concentrate on their supposed weaknesses and ignore the skills they already have. As you move forward, make sure you take a moment to celebrate the achievements you have made, no matter how small or big. Consider the obstacles you've faced, and the things you've learned in the process.

It helps to write down things you know you're good at, accomplishments you've made, etc. It could be achievements in your work life, personal life, or when you stepped outside your comfort zone and conquered your fears. Whenever doubt creeps back in, refer to this list; knowing your strengths reminds you of your capability and helps you reflect upon your ability to tackle new activities.

➢ **Learn from Setbacks**

> Mistakes and setbacks are a part of the journey.

Just because you make a mistake, it doesn't mean the world is coming to an end, but please believe — mistakes and setbacks are a part of the journey. Learn to see failure as a chance to learn and improve instead of a measure of one's value. When things don't go according to plan, ask, "What can I learn from this?" and "What can I do better moving forward?"

If you can change how you look at challenges, you will start viewing them as precious parts of the journey rather than impenetrable walls. That resilience builds your confidence and equips you to approach future hurdles more confidently.

Believe in Yourself

Believing you can achieve great things is the foundation of all self-confidence. This conviction drives every choice you make and every move you execute. Without self-belief, even the most brilliant of plans can crumble beneath the load of doubt.

It's not the same as swagger or acting like you know everything — it's about believing in yourself enough to give it a shot, to fall flat on your face, and to get up and keep moving forward. It's about recognizing your value and owning your dreams. The road to confidence may be challenging, but it is also hugely rewarding.

Bet on Yourself

Betting on yourself is the first step toward the life you've always wanted. It begins by understanding your intrinsic worth and making a promise to yourself to grow. Intrinsic worth is about understanding and accepting that you are valuable simply because you exist—not because of what you do, how others see you, or what you achieve. The promise to grow becomes an act of self-respect rather than self-proving. By acting in the face of uncertainty, recognizing your strengths and embracing failure, you'll build the confidence to help you reach your goals.

Self-confidence isn't merely the foundation of success; it is the fuel that keeps you moving to get there. You will have the belief in yourself to create even greater victories ahead.

Invest in Your Abilities

Betting on yourself means first investing in your personal development, skills, and overall well-being. Investing time, energy, and resources into your own self-improvement prepares you with success tools for the long-term. This isn't indulgence — it's the building blocks you need to create a successful business and life. All your efforts to improve your skills, break the myth of limiting you, and bring you a step closer to being able to achieve everything you have ever wanted.

How to Invest in Yourself

- **Lifelong Learning:** The most successful people do not stop learning. So when the world is continuously changing, keeping up to date and learning becomes a criterion for a competitive atmosphere. Continuous learning enables you to acquire new skills, improve existing ones, and gain knowledge in areas that support your business goals.

- **Discover Free Courses:** Websites such as edX and FutureLearn provide numerous university-level courses at no cost. There's a course for you, whether you want to learn digital marketing, project management or public speaking.

- **The Wisdom in Books:** Books are full of wisdom. They are designed to broaden your mindset and give you some valuable takeaways. There are excellent books available regarding entrepreneurship, leadership, and personal development.

- **Participate in Workshops and Seminars:** Workshops and seminars offer practical experience and the chance to network with industry professionals. They help you to stay motivated and inspired, too. Embracing continuous learning will keep you ahead of the curve and expose you to new opportunities.

- **Networking:** The company you keep is one of the best investments you can make. The people you surround yourself with can affect your outlook, lift you up, and connect you with new opportunities. Networking is more than exchanging business cards — it is developing real relationships that will help you grow.

- **Go to Industry Networking Events:** Conferences, workshops, and meetups are wonderful places to network within your industry. Networking isn't only about what you will receive — it's about what you will also give. Not only does this enhance trust and credibility within your community, but your community sees you giving your knowledge freely and supporting others.

- **Utilize Social Media:** Join groups on sites such as LinkedIn or Facebook that facilitate professional and entrepreneurial idea sharing and collaborations.

- **Gain Invaluable Experience From a Mentor:** A mentor gives you valuable insights and guidance from their own life. Their perspective is a useful guide to common pitfalls and beneficial strategies for getting out of your own way.

Health and Well-Being

Your physical and mental well-being are essential to success. A healthy body and a sharp mind allow you to do your best work. Making time for self-care isn't a luxury — it's a requirement.

➢ **Exercise:** Physical activity increases energy levels, improves focus, and alleviates stress. Even a few minutes a day can help.

➢ **Eat:** A well-balanced diet can energize your body and mind. Incorporate whole, nutrient-rich foods into your meals to sustain energy throughout the day.

➢ **Manage Stress:** Meditation, journaling, and sometimes just getting away can help you maintain focus and ground yourself. Managing stress is important because burnout is a legitimate risk for entrepreneurs.

You need to make yourself a priority because when you are healthy, you can chase your goals with the energy and clarity they require.

Financial Investment

Investing in yourself is usually not free. Investing in tools, training and resources requires setting aside a portion of your income for them, but this can help you reach your goal faster.

- **Buy Tools and Software:** The right tools can help a process flow and make life easier. Find software like project management apps, design tools, and CRM platforms that improve productivity.

- **Work with a coach or consultant:** You may be better off finding a paid coach and getting specific knowledge instead of trial and error. A coach can personalize and design the program according to your needs.

- **Network at Conferences:** You can learn a lot of things at these events, but attendance also opens the chance for you to network with others from the industry.

Consider these expenses investments rather than costs. The dividends you reap—in knowledge, speed, and relationships—far exceed the initial investment.

Every single investment you make in yourself is a step closer to the life you imagine. Every single one of those things moves you a bit closer to an outcome. It's an assertion that you believe in your own possibility and will do what it takes to make it happen.

Investing in yourself is not just preparing for success, it's creating success. The more you grow, the better prepared you'll be for challenges, opportunities, and turning your vision into reality. By prioritizing yourself, you're putting your money into the best investment you'll ever make: you.

I'll never forget the first time I invested over $20K in a business mastermind. I honestly thought I was out of my mind. Who spends that much on training, right? But I decided to take the leap, and looking back, it was one of the best decisions I've ever made for my business.

Two things really stood out from that experience. First, on day one, the coach told us that the first year of the program would be all about shifting our mindsets—becoming the person we needed to be in order to grow our businesses. At first, I couldn't imagine it taking a whole year, but she was absolutely right.

The second takeaway was the proximity to greatness. I met some truly incredible entrepreneurs in that mastermind, and many of them are still part of my network today. These were people making impressive amounts of money every month, but more importantly, they were people I could relate to. The connections were invaluable, and the experience was nothing short of epic.

So, don't be afraid to invest in yourself. That decision gave me a glimpse of what was possible, and it completely changed the trajectory of my business.

How to Maximize Your Workday

Your full-time job doesn't have to get in the way of entrepreneurship. In fact, it can be an advantage. You can grow your business without sacrificing other obligations.

- **Use Breaks Strategically:** Use lunch breaks and down time to brainstorm ideas, respond to emails, or plot out next steps. Even 15 minutes can have an impact.

- **Learn During Idle Time:** If you have a job that involves a lot of repetition and some gaps of waiting, you can always listen to podcasts, audiobooks, and online courses that are related to your business goals.

- **Use Your Work Skills in Your Business:** Make a list of skills you're learning at work that will help your business. For example, If you're gaining experience in marketing, use that knowledge to market your side hustle.

- **Plan Ahead:** Set aside evenings and weekends for tasks related to your own business. Every little thing you do in your day accumulates immediately. Be intentional about your workday and seize every opportunity.

Identifying Limiting Beliefs

Limiting beliefs are the internal forces that prevent you from accessing your full potential. They can block you before you even take a step because they are founded on fear and self-doubt. They often show up as things like:

Limiting beliefs are the internal forces that prevent you from accessing your full potential.

"I don't have enough time."

"I'm not smart enough to start a company.

"I'll fail if I try."

These beliefs become powerful by influencing your actions — or preventing you from taking action altogether. They speak doubts that keep you in your safe spot and deny you exploration beyond your safe spots. When individuals want to bet on themselves and build a successful business, they need to identify these limiting beliefs and overcome them.

How to Eliminate Limiting Beliefs

Acknowledge Them

The first step to overcome your limiting beliefs is to identify them. Many times, these thoughts run in the background of your mind and drive your decision-making without you even being aware of them. Now, take a moment to reflect and be honest with yourself as to what fears or doubts are preventing you from moving forward.

If you need to, write down these thoughts. For example:

"I'm too old to begin something new."

"Not enough experience.'

"I would not be taken seriously."

Writing these beliefs down helps you give them form. That way, you can face them head-on, instead of allowing those sneaky thoughts to continue sabotaging your confidence.

Challenge Them

After you've figured out your limiting beliefs, question if they are objectively true. They're usually based on assumptions or fears rather than facts.

If you think, *I don't have enough time,* take a hard look at how you are spending your day. Are there things, such as mindless scrolling through social media or endless TV watching, that could probably be replaced with something that would further your goal?

Ask yourself:

> *What proof do I have to back up this belief?*

> *Is this belief helping me, or is it hindering me?*

> *What is the worst possible thing that could happen if I just ignored this thought?*

This one mindset is able to expose your limiting beliefs for what they really are — mental barriers, not impossible blocks.

Reframe the Narrative

Once you have questioned your limiting beliefs, the next step is to reframe these limiting beliefs into empowering statements.

That does not mean denying reality, but rather reformulating your mindset to concentrate on possibilities and growth.

For instance:

- Replace "I'll fail if I try" with "Every effort I make brings me closer to success."

- Change "I'm not experienced enough" to "I'm willing to learn what I need to succeed."

- Replace "I don't have enough time" with "I will prioritize my time to focus on what matters most."

Reframing puts you in charge of the narrative and replaces fear with confidence. This helps change your mindset from limitation to opportunity.

Take Action

The best way to break down limiting beliefs is to take them out with evidence. Plan small, intentional steps to build confidence and develop a new empowering story.

For example:

If you think, *I can't launch a business because I don't understand very much,* enroll in a free class or read a book on developing a business.

If you think, *I'm not good at networking*, try going to a small event and introducing yourself to just one person.

Set up a small, achievable goal and celebrate all steps you take toward that goal.

Every step you take, even the little ones, builds confidence that you can face something difficult. Every time you confront your doubts through action, those doubts become less powerful.

The Power of Limiting Beliefs Being Challenged

When you challenge a limiting belief, you can pronounce yourself a better person. You discover that fear and doubt are not iron-clad barriers but hurdles that can be vaulted with intention and work.

Betting on yourself is the belief that you are capable of succeeding — and that belief gets stronger every time you prove it to yourself. But when you acknowledge, challenge, reframe, and act on your limiting beliefs, you can finally release those mental constraints that have kept you stuck in place for so long, and you can take steps toward your goals, feeling confident and clear.

Building a Growth Mindset

Having a growth mindset means that you believe you can improve your skills, abilities, and intelligence through effort, learning, and perseverance. It's an inspiring way of thinking that makes you view obstacles as chances to develop instead of as stumbling blocks to achievement. The growth mindset is imperative for entrepreneurs since it encourages resilience, adaptability, and the capacity to learn from their failures — all traits that are fundamental when starting and growing your own company.

A growth mindset is the belief that success comes from hard work and learning. Unlike the fixed mindset, which assumes that talent and intelligence are "fixed" (you either have it or you don't), the growth mindset empowers you with the philosophy that you can improve and grow as long as you are willing to learn and work hard. It's not about your genetics; it's about how much work you're willing to put in.

The path of entrepreneurship is littered with uncertainty, challenges, and self-doubt. When you develop a growth mindset, you are able to navigate through those challenges by focusing on learning and growth rather than perfection. It enables you to pivot with shifting conditions, recover from adversity and tackle challenges with curiosity and creativity.

For example, an individual with a fixed mindset may view a marketing campaign that failed to generate the desired results as a failure in and of itself and lose motivation as a result. On the other hand, a person with a growth mindset would reflect on what did not go as planned, extract lessons from it and fire it up again with an enhanced approach.

Embrace Challenges

Challenges are a common theme in every entrepreneurial journey, and they don't have to be seen as a negative thing. Rather, view them as a chance to learn new things and develop your skills further. Each of your challenges teaches you something—whether it's about your business, your market, or you.

So if you're struggling to build a social media presence for your business, look at it as a chance to learn digital marketing skills or get to know your audience better. Challenges are not obstacles that lead to giving up; they are steppingstones to greater accomplishments.

Ask yourself:

"What does this situation have to teach me?"

"How is this challenge going to make me stronger?"

This prism guides your sight toward what is possible rather than what you feel is no longer achievable, motivating you day after day despite the tough times.

Celebrate Progress

One of the most frequent traps for entrepreneurs is being overly focused on the destination and not sufficiently focused on the journey. Having a growth mindset requires us to recognize and rejoice in every step forward, no matter how tiny!

Success takes more than one night. Identifying your incremental wins helps you stay motivated and gain momentum. For instance, be proud of milestones such as allowing a website to go live, getting your first customer or finalizing a difficult project.

Perfectionism implies that nothing less than flawless execution is ever sufficient, which is too often a path to burnout or worse, paralysis. You are closing the distance between you and your big goals with every little step you take.

Seek Feedback

Monitoring feedback can be one of the most impactful growth opportunities you'll ever come across — unless you don't wish to hear it. Constructive criticism helps you notice blind spots, improve your method, and achieve better outcomes. Do not make feedback something you are afraid of; turn it into a lesson and learn from it.

> Do not make feedback something you are afraid of; turn it into a lesson and learn from it.

For example, if a client gives you constructive criticism regarding your product or service, don't take it personally. Let their feedback guide how you improve. Likewise, consult with mentors, peers or industry professionals who can give valuable advice.

This is a key part of developing a growth mindset: being willing to hear feedback so you know how to learn and change your ways.

Focus on the Journey

The road to success takes time and is seldom a straight line. Learning about a growth mindset is being inspired by the journey instead of fixating on the end goal. It is also important to understand that every experience (whether you define it as a success or a failure) contains lessons that you can only gain through that experience, and they help you grow.

So, for instance, even if your business fails to meet its revenue targets during the first year, focus on what you learned about your market, your operations, your strategies, and so on. You will learn lessons that will set you up for success later on.

Focusing on the journey helps you learn to be patient and persistent, both key attributes of long-term success.

In cultivating a growth mindset, you remain optimistic and persistent, even in the face of uncertainty regarding what lies ahead. It enables you to see failure not as a personal flaw but as a central piece of the learning experience. This is the kind of mindset that helps you function at an optimum level while evolving and growing as a person and in your business in good and bad times.

By opening yourself to challenges, celebrating progress, seeking feedback, and enjoying the journey, you will cultivate the resilience and adaptability necessary to succeed as an entrepreneur. Success is not always a straight path, and with a growth mindset, you will view each twist and turn as an opportunity to learn and grow.

Make the most of your job. Your 9-to-5 doesn't need to be an obstacle to entrepreneurship; it can be the very thing that launches you into it. For many aspiring entrepreneurs, the 9-to-5 is something to be overcome, a shackled state from which one must escape before chasing the dream. By reframing your thinking, however, you can view your job as a means to help you create a safety net while building your business.

The job gives you experience, contacts, and some capital — all without expecting income to come out of the door immediately. Use what your job provides to set you up for an easier transition into being an entrepreneur.

Ways to Leverage Your Job

<u>Gain Experience</u>

If you are working for someone else, use it as a classroom to learn skills in your industry and gain knowledge that you can directly use in your business. The tasks you complete at work every day — whether project management, client communication or problem-solving — are transferable to your entrepreneurial pursuits.

Here are some examples:

Project Management: If your role includes managing timelines and coordinating teams, you're acquiring critical experience managing the organization and execution of tasks, which is integral to running a business.

Customer Service: Working with customers helps you learn to understand customer needs, respond to feedback and manage conflict.

Financial Management: Whether it's budgeting for your department or keeping tabs on expenses at work, you've done financial management of the sort that can set you up for handling your business finances.

Seek opportunities to bring the business aspect to the skills you're already using at work. Think of your job as a training ground that is setting you up for your foray into entrepreneurship.

Build Relationships

Networking opportunities are plentiful in the workplace. Your co-workers, clients, and vendors could be vital connections as you grow your business. Some might become customers, business partners or potential mentors to coach you.

Here's how to network strategically:

Colleagues: Tell **trusted co-workers** about your goals. People may have skills or resources that could help you, or they might introduce you to others in their network.

Clients and Vendors: If your business idea is related to your current industry, your business connections can help you find partners or opportunities.

Mentors: Seek out experienced individuals within the office who will offer advice on overcoming challenges or scaling your business.

Networking is not simply about requesting assistance; it's about nurturing relationships in which your connection and the person you reach out to each benefit from the other's success.

Fund Your Dream

Financial stability is one of the best things about a full-time job. It can help you finance things like marketing tools, website hosting, or product development without going through loans or outside investors.

There are ways that you can use your income to the best of your abilities. You should allocate some money from your salary for business expenses.

- **Buy tools and resources:** Buy software, training or equipment that you can use to grow your business.

- **Save for Big Expenses:** Create a financial cushion for large future expenses, like product launches or hiring assistance.

- **Test Ideas:** Try out small projects or side hustles in the evening, on weekends, or in your spare time. This approach allows you to hone your ideas, understand your market, and gain confidence before going all-in on entrepreneurship. For example:

  - **Freelancing:** Provide your services on a small scale and test for demand.

  - **Prototyping**: Build a replica of your product to collect feedback from target customers.

  - **Side Hustles:** Start with low-risk options, like selling on Etsy or creating digital products, to gauge what your audience responds to.

Finding out what works and what doesn't allows you to minimize risks and maximize your chances of success, all while keeping your "job stability" intact.

Your job is the steppingstone for successfully building a business. It provides financial stability, opportunities to develop skills, and a network of professional connections, all of which can be utilized for the acceleration of your career/decisions. Seeing your job as a partner and not an enemy helps you create smart moves that champion you for the upcoming successes ahead.

So don't rush into quitting your job; put your job to work for you — use it to fund your dreams, learn skills, and test your ideas. With the right mindset and approach, your job can actually be a crucial aspect of your entrepreneurial journey.

Exercises to Build Confidence

Here are practical exercises to reinforce your confidence and silence doubt:

- **Daily Visualization:** Take a couple of minutes a day to visualize that you are achieving your goals. Visualize the actions you'll take and the benefits you'll reap.

- **Track Achievements:** Make a note of any successes you create, no matter how small. Reflecting on your progress shows you what you are capable of.

- **Set Micro-Goals:** Break down large, overwhelming goals into tiny, doable things. This creates momentum and confidence.

- **Study Role Models:** Study entrepreneurs who began in similar circumstances to yours. Their stories can inspire and motivate you.

How to Bet on Yourself: Actionable Strategies

Betting on yourself is moving forward on the dream day after day. Here are some strategies to help you focus:

> ➤ **Create a Vision Board:** Put up images, quotes and goals that reflect your dreams. Put it somewhere you will see it every day.

> ➤ **Schedule "You Time":** Schedule specific time to work on your business. Make it a non-negotiable appointment.

> ➤ **Celebrate Wins:** Celebrate milestones, such as launching your website or making your first sale.

> ➤ **Stay Accountable:** Talk to a trusted friend, mentor, or accountability group about your goals.

> ➤ **Work harder for yourself:** Betting on yourself is having faith that you can forge a better path ahead. It's about realizing that the energy you expend doing your job can be redirected to creating something meaningful for yourself. By investing in your growth, fighting against your own doubts and making the most of your time, you can take the first steps to reaching financial independence.

Stop working harder for someone else's dream, and work harder for yours—it's time.

The path isn't always easy, but each small step you take brings you closer to the life that you dream of. Stop working harder for someone else's dream, and work harder for yours—it's time.

CHAPTER 3
Escape Strategically: Make the Most of Your Paid Leave

With limited time and energy available for your new venture, working a full-time job while building a business means you have to be creative, dedicated, and strategic about how much you devote to the business. However, one of the most underutilized resources for aspiring entrepreneurs is paid leave. Vacation days, personal days and other leave are powerful tools that can allow you to carve out dedicated time for your business without damaging the financial cushion provided by your 9-to-5. This chapter will address how to best utilize this time, ensure you're prioritizing correctly, and achieve impactful advancement toward your goals.

The True Value of Paid Leave

Paid leave is often associated with relaxation and rejuvenation, and although you need to rest, such leave can also be a moment to drive your business forward. A few days of undistracted focus can keep your big-ticket items moving, set the stage for projects just over the horizon and create some momentum. When you use your leave deliberately, you turn it from a break into an investment in your journey as an entrepreneur.

Consider your paid leave a new secret weapon in your business toolkit. It enables you to give these tasks the full attention that they might take weeks to achieve in the limited hours following a workday. Use one day off strategically to make the biggest difference.

Planning Your Paid Leave To Create The Most Impact

Without a plan, paid leave can be lost for good, with little to show for any effort spent. Proper planning allows you to maximize this time and accomplish what you set out to do.

How to Strategically Plan Your Leave

- **Define Your Objectives:** The first step is figuring out what you'd like to do during your time off. Be it starting your website, building a product, or formulating a marketing strategy, having goals in place makes sure that you stay focused.

- **Prioritize Tasks:** Make a list of all that you want to accomplish and prioritize tasks. Concentrate on whatever will propel your business forward most effectively.

- **Break Tasks into Steps:** It can be daunting with a big project. Breaking tasks into steps can make them more manageable, actionable and measurable to help ensure that you stay on track.

- **Create a Detailed Schedule:** Use your leave as chunks of time for particular tasks. For instance, spend your mornings on higher-energy tasks, such as thinking time or writing time, and your afternoons on administrative work.

- **Prepare in Advance:** Collect all the tools, materials and resources you will need before your leave starts. This is to avoid wasting time. Planning ahead ensures that every day of your leave will be focused on your business goals.

- **Use Time-Blocking for Productivity:** Time-blocking is an essential strategy for maximizing productivity during your leave. It focuses on breaking down your work into fixed time blocks, to help you stay more structured and focused.

  What Is Time-Blocking and How to Do It:

  - **Start with Priorities:** Complete your most important tasks at the times of the day you are most awake and energized. For many, mornings are great for creativity and strategy.

  - **Break Down Projects:** Break down big projects into small chunks. So you might break down "Build website" into time blocks like "Choose a domain name," "Write homepage content," and "Set up hosting."

  - **Include Breaks**: Set up short periods of rest and recharge. This will keep you from burning out and allows you to continue working at a high caliber throughout your day.

- ○ **Review and Adjust:** At the close of each day take stock of what you've accomplished and reschedule if need be. Flexibility is needed to maintain your progress. Time-blocking keeps you productive and helps you make the most of each precious hour of your leave.

- ○ **Merging Weekends with Holidays, as Well as Paid Leave:** Paid leave isn't the only tool you have for focused time on your business. Combining leave days with weekends and public holidays means longer stretches of uninterrupted time.

Ways to Do More with the Time You Have

- • **Long Weekends:** Take a vacation day on a Friday or Monday, combining it with the weekend for three consecutive days of productivity. Additional time gives you the room to take on larger projects, or get multiple things done.

- • **Public Holidays:** Schedule major business activities on holidays you're not working. These days are great for deep, high-impact work.

- • **Weekend Focus Blocks:** Schedule dedicated times to work on your business over the weekends (e.g., Saturday mornings or Sunday evenings). Persistent efforts compound over time. You create space to work without burning yourself out.

Job Responsibilities Balancing

Even as you use your leave time to focus on your business, it's critical to still stay true to your job performance. Your full-time job pays for your own entrepreneurial venture anyway, right?

Tips to Balance between Work and Business

- **Communicate Clearly:** If you are going to take leave for any work purposes. Make sure your absence will be accounted for.

- **Set Boundaries:** You devote the majority of your leave to your business. Likewise, when you're at work, focus on your work.

- **Stay Organized:** Use calendars, task managers and project management tools to keep track of deadlines and commitments.

It takes discipline and planning to balance work and business, but it's doable with the right mindset.

Examples of Using Leave Strategically in Real Life

Seeing the successes of others who have successfully used their leave can inspire you and guide your own efforts. Here are a few examples of how entrepreneurs made the most of their time off:

- **Building a Website:**
  A teacher built a professional website for their tutoring

business over holiday break. They employed time-blocking to write content, design pages, and establish booking systems — all steps they took to prepare for future growth.

- **Creating a Business Plan:**
  One accountant spent a three-day weekend developing a comprehensive business plan that included financial projections, marketing strategies and a roadmap for the business's first year in operation.

- **Scaling a Side Hustle:**
  The software engineer spent their time off preparing to improve their freelance app development practice. They concentrated on networking with clients, bringing their portfolio up to date, and automating mundane tasks.

These narratives highlight how judicious use of paid leave can help achieve major milestones, even for those holding down a full-time job.

Focus More on the Most Important Tasks

Some tasks add value to your business more than others. So as you step away, focus on high impact things that deliver results and lay the groundwork for lasting success.

Examples of High-Impact Activities:

- **Creating Products:** You can create income-generating digital courses, eBooks, or physical products.

- **Marketing and Promotion:** Schedule social media campaigns, craft email newsletters, or configure ads that will appear in front of your audience.

- **Networking:** Arrange meetings with prospective clients, collaborators or mentors who can help take your business forward.

- **Market Research:** Use this time to research your target market, your competitors, and your business model. Focusing on these activities will ensure that your efforts produce meaningful results.

Preventing burnout

Working for long periods of time can be hard, even if you care a lot about your business. Here are several ways to prevent burnout.

- **Set Achievable Milestones:**
  Set small goals and celebrate every small step you take to achieve them.

- **Reward Yourself:**
  Reward yourself for getting through big things. A little reward can motivate you and keep you going.

- **Surround Yourself with Inspiration:**
  Have inspirational quotes, success stories or podcasts close to you to keep you on your path ambitiously.

- **Minimize Distractions:**
  Do not disturb: Mute notifications, set a physical work-space and tell people around you that you need time.

The key is to balance work and rest, so that you remain productive and not burnt out.

Evaluate Your Progress

End your leave with some reflection on what you've done. Assessing your progress also gets you to think about what worked, what didn't, and how you want to grow in the future.

Questions to Reflect On:

> **Did I Achieve My Goals?**
> Take a look at your goals and see how far you've come.

> **What Worked Well?**
> Find strategies and approaches that worked

> **What Can I Improve?**
> Identify sectors that gave you the most trouble and consider what you should do differently the next time you tackle that area.

What's Next?

Now that you've gained some momentum, use that to make plans for your next moves.

Reflection ensures that you are always learning and growing, so each period of leave is more productive than the one before.

Personal Insights: My Journey

In my case, paid leave was key to building my publishing business. I took vacation days to finalize everything: writing copy for my website, creating contracts, developing marketing strategies, and connecting with authors and entrepreneurs. Through proper time management and techniques such as time-blocking, I found myself completing a lot in a short time.

One time that really made an impression on me was a chain of four days in a row that I spent with a business mastermind group, learning new skills, implementing systems and investing time and money to learn and network with other high-achieving entrepreneurs. Day one was focused on branding, day two on content creation, day three on email marketing, and day four on launch planning. This dedicated time allowed me to learn in just a few days what would have taken weeks, months or years trying to accomplish on evenings and weekends.

Paid leave, alongside weekends and holidays, became integral to my plan, because it gave me the means to build my business without sacrificing my full-time job.

Conclusion: Transforming Time into Progress

Your paid time off is a superpower. Used wisely, it can rapidly accelerate your entrepreneurial journey without derailing your work or personal life. With some foresight, some smart prioritization, and sufficient motivation, you can transform your leave into significant steps forward.

Every little bit of time counts; just keep at it. Any time you take away from your job to focus on your business, whether it be a week of vacation, a day off, or a long weekend, you are making progress toward your idea of success.

CHAPTER 4
Build Your Dream Team: Keep Your Business Thriving While You Clock In

If you are working a full-time job, you surely will need some support to run your business. You can't do it all yourself and attempting to balance everything will result in burnout. In fact, having a trustworthy team is critical for keeping your business on course even when your attention is divided. Delegation, hiring help, and consistent communication are secrets to making sure your business survives and grows while you do the time.

The Value of Delegation

Many people think of delegation as a requirement in large companies, but for the entrepreneur, it's a superpower. Delegation is not just about assigning tasks — it's about intentionally reallocating tasks so you can spend time where it matters in your business. Doing so ensures that you can concentrate on what really matters:

helping your business grow and paving its way toward sustained success.

In their quest for success, entrepreneurs often fall into the trap of doing everything alone, particularly in the infancy of their business. Even though it might appear the path that is most affordable or efficient, you come to find that this way of thinking creates burnout and seizes potential. But delegation is what helps your business to grow past your individual limits, taking it where it needs to be.

Why Delegation Is Essential

Time Efficiency

For entrepreneurs, time is one of the most precious resources. But a lot of business owners find themselves mired in administrative tasks, day-to-day operations or petty details that don't need their involvement. Outsource these jobs, and you take back time you can devote to the areas where you offer your best skills.

For instance, if you spend hours managing your emails or updating your website, you can simply outsource those tasks to a virtual assistant or freelancer. It enables you to focus on strategic planning, client acquisition, or product development — activities that directly contribute to your business growth.

Skill Leverage

You don't need to be an expert at everything as a business owner. Delegation is one of the most powerful benefits because it allows you to tap into others' skill(s) and expertise. This will allow you to enhance the quality of your own business output, improving outcomes for your customers.

For instance:

A graphic designer can design marketing materials which resonate with your audience at a professional level.

With the help of a social media manager, you can create motivating content to help you expand your online presence.

So when you delegate to skilled individuals, not only does it make your work better, it also allows you to get it done sooner and more effectively than if you were attempting to do it all yourself.

Business Growth

Delegating is fundamental to the scaled growth of your business. It doesn't matter how talented or hardworking you are, you're limited by how many hours you have in a day. But to expand and grow your business, you need a team that can help you manage the increased demand and find you more clients or products to sell.

Through creating a dependable team, an individual is capable of multiplying their work and getting stuff done in less time. Delegation allows you to concentrate on business leadership, innovation and strategic decisions—the roles that only you can fill as owner of the business. Your team can also take care of the daily functioning of your business so that everything runs as usual, even when you're not actively in the picture.

Getting Past Obstacles to Delegation

Though its beneficial, many entrepreneurs struggle to delegate due to common fears, such as the fear of losing control, fear about cost or the fear that no one is able to do the job the same as they can. It can also be helpful to acknowledge that these barriers may require a change in mindset to allow others to take some responsibility.

Here's how to start:

Delegate Small Tasks: Assign simple, low-risk tasks to build group trust and confidence.

Set Clear Expectations: Clearly communicate deliverables and define key metrics for success, which ultimately sets your team members up to succeed.

Outcome-Driven: Treat delegation like an investment that will free up your time and energy for high-impact activities that yield better returns.

Even though delegation takes effort, time, and resources at the beginning, the long-term benefits are well worth the short-term investment. Freeing yourself from the things that others can do (and do well) gives you time to spend on growing your business and hitting targets.

Delegation doesn't mean giving up control; rather, it is transferring some control to allow others to help realize your vision, creating a business that is both scalable and sustainable — and doing that by building a team and giving them enough trust to manage their own responsibilities. Just remember this one simple rule: When you delegate more of your work, your business can grow, thrive and succeed.

Identifying Tasks to Delegate

The smallest part of delegation is determining what to delegate. Start by asking yourself:

- What are the most time-consuming tasks that don't need my involvement?

- What skills do I not possess that somebody else can provide?

- What tasks are repetitive and can be streamlined?

Tasks you can delegate include:

Administrative Tasks: Managing emails, scheduling, and data entry.

Blog Creation: Writers, designers, video editors.

Customer Support: Answering questions or dealing with social media messages.

Technical Tasks: Website updates, app development, or IT support

When you focus on what only you can do — whether that is strategic planning, decision-making, pitching ideas, or building relationships with clients — you'll be making the best use of your time.

Building a Support Network

Your dream team doesn't necessarily need to be made up of full-time employees. Most entrepreneurs begin by employing freelancers, contractors, or part-time collaborators. This is an economical and practical arrangement that allows you the flexibility to tap into talent without the attached long-term overhead.

Here's how to create a dependable support system:

Define Roles Clearly: Make it clear what you need help with, what you want your team to be responsible for. This ensures you will find the right person for the job.

Key: Start Small — Recruit one or two people for the main business sections that need filling.

Seek Recommendations: Reach out to colleagues or mentors for suggestions. Reliable collaborators are often found through trusted referrals.

Using Online Platforms: Sites such as Upwork, Fiverr and Freelancer enable you to hire skilled workers of varying degrees of experience and price.

Note that your network isn't just paid collaborators. Friends, family, or peers might also be willing to offer support, advice or resources.

Hiring on a Budget

It doesn't have to cost an arm and a leg to build a team; with proper planning, you can find affordable options to suit your needs.

Here are some strategies:

Outsource Specific Projects: Rather than bringing someone in to work for you long-term, hire freelancers on a contract basis for specific tasks, such as designing your logo or building a website.

Tap Internships: Advertise internships for students or recent graduates wanting to get experience. Make sure this is a win-win situation.

Trade: Use barter services to trade your services/products for something you need. If you're a marketer, provide promotional support in exchange for design work, etc.

Embrace Automation: Automate the repetitive tasks via automation tools to minimize manual effort.

Beginning small helps you to identify what is most effective for your enterprise while keeping costs in check.

Staying In Touch and Feeling Accountable

Great administration involves clear communication and accountability. Without these, tasks can slip through the cracks with frustrating and potentially disastrous consequences. Here's how to keep your team aligned and productive:

Set Expectations: Define goals, deadlines, and deliverables clearly for each team member. Once you've agreed, document it to avoid misunderstandings.

Select communication tools: Slack, Zoom, or Asana are a few options that help keep you connected and organized.

Schedule Regular Check-ins: Have weekly or bi-weekly meetings to share updates and challenges and hold everyone accountable.

Mentor: Guide your team and help them grow as a group. Keep morale high by celebrating successes.

Track Performance: Use tools like Trello, ClickUp, or Monday.com to track progress and hold yourselves accountable.

Consistency is key. By remaining engaged and supportive you will ensure your team is motivated and productive.

Building a Culture of Trust

Trust is the bedrock of any cohesive team. When your team members feel valued and trusted, they are more inclined to take ownership of their work and help your business succeed.

Here's how to build trust:

Be More Transparent: Be open and share your vision, goals, and expectations.

Leverage Your Team: Trust team members to make decisions within their scope.

Express Gratitude: Show appreciation for your team's efforts, both publicly and privately.

Be Reliable: Honor your commitments and uphold your standards as you would demand of your team.

These actions set up a foundation of success and everyone is highly engaged.

My Experience with Creating My Dream Team

When I began my publishing business, I wanted to do everything myself but the reality was, writing copy, designing book covers, and creating websites for our authors was not my strong suit. It started to feel overwhelming, and I knew I couldn't do it all alone.

I started out hiring a freelance graphic designer to make book covers. She was also great with layout and design for our books. It freed up hours of my time and drastically improved the quality of our products. Then I hired an executive assistant who helped me with admin work so that I could build more on the operational side.

Forming my team wasn't an instant process. I began small and grew my network over time. Today, I have a team of talented individuals who cover everything from editing, design and formatting to photography (capturing professional headshots for our authors). Their work has been crucial to the success of my business.

How to Scale Your Team as Your Business Scales

When your business grows, your team will need to grow too. When scaling your team, it takes lots of planning to ensure that you are hiring the right people at the right cadence.

Let's see how to scale properly:

Anticipate Needs: Determine the growing needs for additional support as your business evolves.

Support Learning: Ensure there is money/funding available to train new team members.

Review Regularly: Check in periodically to see how the team is doing and make adjustments as needed.

With an increased number of team members comes a greater scope of projects, a larger customer base and heightened company success.

Anticipated Challenges and How to Address Them

Forming a team is not without its pain points. Some common problems and solutions are:

Finding the Right Fit: Spend time vetting candidates thoroughly. Hold interviews, check portfolios and request references.

Remote Teams: Keep remote teams aligned using collaboration tools and clear communication protocols.

Cost-accounting: Hire contractors. Seek part-time arrangements or freelancers until you are fully able to meet your needs.

Note: Always remember quality, having high standards and clear instructions which give the same output every time.

There is a lesson in every challenge that will contribute to building an even better team.

A Final Thought: Remember, You've Got a Team!

Your team is the most important part of your business. With delegation, smart hiring and communication, you can create a team that believes in your vision and helps you grow your business. And remember, you don't have to do it all by yourself. When you have the right people surrounding you, you are limitless.

As you can see, building a team requires some time, effort, and trust, but in return, it is incredibly rewarding. Assess the trouble spot, bring in your dream team, then listen to what they say. Start small and keep it tight, and your business will grow.

CHAPTER 5
Set It and Forget It: Build Automated Systems

It's no easy feat to juggle running a business and a full-time job. The secret to making it doable — and successful — is developing systems that work for you, even when your plate is full with other commitments. Automation solutions and simplified processes minimize manual effort, save time, and keep your business up and running. You'll learn in this chapter how to create fail-proof systems that have you spending time on growing, not doing.

The Importance of Automation

One of the most powerful weapons in a founder's arsenal today is automation. Automation takes care of all the little repetitive tasks and gives you more time and energy to spend on high-value activities that require creativity, problem-solving and strategic thinking. Automation isn't only about being more efficient — it's about developing systems that enable your business to function as it should when you're not in the trenches.

When many entrepreneurs first start their business, they want to do everything by hand. Although this can work perhaps for a time, it's not sustainable on an increasingly larger business. Automation is one of the best types of investment you can make to help you grow, minimize errors, and streamline your operations — making it essential to your long-term success.

Key Benefits of Automation

Time Savings

The time saved is one of the most immediate and tangible benefits of automation. The right tools can do in seconds what takes hours normally. For example:

Social Media Scheduling: Rather than posting updates daily, you can schedule weeks' worth of content in advance with tools like Buffer, or Hootsuite

Automate Email Marketing: Through platforms like Mailchimp, ConvertKit, or Keap, you can set up automated email campaigns, sequences, and follow-ups without having to do anything manually.

Invoicing and Payments: With tools like QuickBooks, Stripe, or PayPal, you can automate invoicing and payment tracking, taking away the headache of manual bookkeeping.

Automating these mundane tasks allows you to dedicate yourself to expanding your business instead of being caught up in daily operations.

Mistakes can happen, particularly when we are all wearing so many hats. Automation decreases possible errors through developing repetitive and trustable systems.

This accuracy provided by automated tools can ensure that customer details are entered correctly, invoices are sent out on time, and email campaigns are personalized and error free.

For instance, customer relationship management (CRM) tools such as Salesforce or HubSpot maintain records of interactions so that no client is forgotten or handled poorly.

Not only does this spare you many a headache, but it also builds your professional reputation and customer experience.

Scalability

With your business growth come the accompanying responsibilities. Manual processes that worked when demand was low become overwhelming as demand goes up. Automation will help your business do more with less.

For instance:

E-commerce automation — Platforms such as Shopify can automate inventory management, order fulfillment and customer communication.

Project Management Tools: Tools such as Asana or Trello allow you to easily manage progress on projects and assignments that get delegated among team members, even as that team grows.

When you build scalable systems from the beginning, you prepare your business for growth without compromising quality or efficiency.

Customer Support: Using services like Zendesk or Intercom, chatbots provide instant replies to customer questions, available 24/7 with no extra employees.

Lead Generation: Automatic lead-capturing forms and follow-up emails make it easier to turn website visitors into customers.

Analytics and Reporting: Solutions such as Google Analytics allow you to automate data collection and reporting, providing real-time data about your company performance.

These applications illustrate how deploying automation can simplify complex processes, enabling your business to run better.

Investing in Automation Early

Automating tasks you repeat on a daily basis can help you save numerous hours and headaches in the future, so make sure you invest in the right systems and automation tools as soon as you can in your business. While there's an up-front cost, the time and energy savings are well worth the investment. Automation tools will save you time and effort and will leave you with peace of mind as you know that some very crucial aspects of your business are under control.

Getting Started with Automation

Identify Repetitive Tasks: Make a list of the tasks you do over and over again such as email responses, appointment scheduling, or order processing.

Find the Right Tools: Find automation tools that suit your exact needs but also stay within budget. There are plenty of free or inexpensive options available for small businesses.

Create Workflows: Set up automation workflow tools according to your needs.

Monitor and Optimize: Periodically check in on the automated processes to ensure they are operating per design and enhancing efficiency in your operations.

Automation — The Future of Your Business

Automation isn't just a nice-to-have for Fortune 500 companies — it's a necessity for businesses large and small. By automating repetitive tasks, you have more time to pay attention to things that actually matter for business: innovation, strategy, and customer relationships. Automation also sets your business up for growth, allowing it to scale without drowning in operational demands.

Investing early ensures you're not only saving time, but you're also building a sustainable system that is sure to help your business' success over the long haul.

Essential Areas to Automate

You can apply automation to many parts of your business. Here are some important things to follow:

Scheduling and Calendar Management: Work with different tools to plan appointments, meetings, and social media posts. Tools like Google Calendar and Calendly simplify the process of organizing time and sharing availability.

Email Marketing: Send automated email sequences and continue to engage with your leads through a tool like Mailchimp, Convert Kit or Active Campaign.

Social media management tools: Platforms including Buffer, Hootsuite, and Later that allow you to create, plan, schedule, and publish posts across social media channels.

Customer Relationship Management (CRM): Tools such as HubSpot or Zoho allow you to track customer interactions, manage leads and streamline communication.

For Payment Processing and Invoicing: Solutions such as PayPal, Stripe, or QuickBooks can enable you to accept payments, send invoices, and maintain your finances with ease.

Cloud Storage: The cloud organizes and stores your files on platforms like Google Drive or Dropbox, making them accessible from anywhere.

Automating these areas can help significantly cut down on the time spent on administrative tasks.

TOOLS & PLATFORMS EXAMPLES

Automation has been transformational in my publishing business. Here are some tools I, my teammates, and my colleagues use for operational efficiency:

Canva — Easy for you to create eye-catching graphics for your marketing and branding.

Keap (Email Marketing): Keap is great for automating email campaigns, sending out newsletters, and tracking engagement metrics, among a host of other things.

Trello (Project Management): Trello is excellent for task management, progress monitoring, and team collaboration.

Google Workspace (Collaboration): Google Docs and Google Sheets simplify file sharing, effective collaboration in real time, and general organization.

Zapier (Workflow Automation) Zapier integrates various apps, easily automating processes such as syncing email leads with CRMs or sending notifications.

These platforms allow small businesses to communicate easily, quickly, and cost-effectively.

Establishing Processes with Reduced Human Intervention

It takes planning to have systems in place and running smoothly. Here's a walkthrough of how to implement fail-proof processes:

Scan for Repetitive Tasks: Write down the list of tasks you do repeatedly (for example, answering queries, posting on your social media, or sending out invoices).

Select the Proper Tools: Explore automation tools that fit your requirements. Choose integrated platforms for a smoother workflow.

Design Templates: You can create them for emails, social media posts, contracts, and more, to help you save time. Templates save time and roadblocks.

Create a Roadmap: You will need a place where everything is organized and listed clearly. That makes it easier for others to take things off your plate or to better organize your systems.

Test & Optimize: Simulate your systems before going live to discover wrinkles. Make adjustments to increase both efficiency and reliability.

Monitor and Update: Continuously monitor your systems to make sure they are operating as they should. Improve the tools and processes as your business grows.

These steps will allow you to implement systems that alleviate your workload and improve your business operations.

Automating Customer Interaction

Enhancing customer engagement is one of the most effective ways to use automation. Here's how to work with automation to truly connect with your audience:

Automated Welcome Emails – Create welcome emails for new subscribers. This builds a strong first impression and familiarizes them with your company.

Follow-Up sequences: Email sequences that follow up with the leads.

Social Media Interaction: Automate posts and use third-party tools to monitor comments, messages and mentions. Always reply in a timely manner to strengthen relationships.

Customer Surveys: Automate surveys to collect feedback and insights. It's easy to do this with platforms like Google Forms or Typeform.

Mark Your CRM: Use CRMs to push targeted offers.

With automation, you can still connect with your audience meaningfully while skipping out on having to do it manually.

How to Get Over Most Common Automation Challenges

Although automation can bring many advantages, it is not without its challenges. Here's what to do about some common problems:

Learning Curve: Invest in understanding how your tools work. The majority of platforms have tutorials, guides and customer service.

Cost: Begin with free or inexpensive tools. As your business expands you can switch over to paid features.

Over-Automation: Do not automate personal aspects of your business, like responding to sensitive customer questions. Balance efficiency with authenticity.

System Improvement: Seamless integration of any tools ensures no mess. Apps can be connected with something like Zapier.

By overcoming these hurdles, you'll supercharge the performance of your automated systems.

Streamlining Your Workflow

Streamlining isn't only an automation effort, but a creation of workflows that ease time restraints and lower complication. Here are more tips for clearing the clutter:

Join Similar Tasks: Look for similar tasks that you can group. For instance, batch all of your social media posts for the week in one sitting.

Assign Due Dates: Create deadlines for tasks to add some pressure and organization to the process.

Reduce Decision-Making: Automate decisions using checklists or templates.

Remove Unnecessary Steps: Go through your processes from time to time and discard those steps that do not add value.

A more efficient workflow gives you more time for what truly matters and less busy work.

Staying Flexible

> Not all tasks can or should be automated, and certain tasks need the human touch.

Automation is powerful but remember to keep it loose. Not all tasks can or should be automated, and certain tasks need the human touch. Continue to watch the systems and step in, if necessary.

That flexibility is what will keep your business from getting stuck yet allow it to run on autopilot.

The Takeaway: The Magic of the Foolproof System

Foolproof systems are a game changer for any entrepreneur. With automation and processes, you could create a business that runs like a well-oiled machine without you having to be there. Automation tools like these can allow your team to free up time, you have fewer mistakes in your process, and you can focus on growth and strategy rather than day-to-day operations.

As a reminder, automation is not aiming to take your job; the point is to empower your ability. And with the right systems in place, you can ultimately do more in less time, which sets you up for long-term success. So keep it small, test your processes, and let the business start growing.

CHAPTER 6
Love It or Leave It: Passion Over Paychecks

In business, success is about more than just money — it's about building a life you love. Being able to build a business that is aligned with your personal interests and passions makes the journey not just more enjoyable but increases your odds of success in the long run. This brings out a passion that comes through in your message and the relationships you develop with your fans. This chapter covers why passion is important, how to maintain it, and how to keep the tank filled even in dark times.

It is important to pick a business that resonates with your interests and beliefs. But passion is the fire that drives commitment, creativity, and resilience. Absent this, the most lucrative endeavors can seem like a chore.

Here's why passion is key:

Continuous Motivation: Passion is what drives you, particularly when the going gets tough.

Authors who care about their readers and audience come across as more relatable, as customers can recognize when you are authentic.

Innovation: Passionate people tend to explore new ideas and find new solutions.

Fulfillment: Success feels more satisfying if it's connected to something you love.

Those financial goals are important, but they shouldn't short-circuit the need for personal satisfaction and meaning from your work.

Finding Your Passion

If you're still not sure what kind of business suits your passion, start by asking yourself the following questions:

- What activities cause me to lose track of time?
- What do I love to learn about or talk about?
- What skills or hobbies make me happy?
- What problems am I inspired to solve?

Your answers can help steer you toward business ideas that align with your interests and strengths. For example:

- If you're passionate about cooking, launch a catering service or food blog, or start a recipe subscription.

- If you like teaching, look into online courses, coaching, or tutoring.

- Creative thinkers can design products, write or create digital content.

Your passion doesn't need to be earth-shattering; it just needs to be aligned with who you are and what you love.

How to Keep Your Zest Without Losing Your Mind

Even when you have a passion for your business, there are times when motivation slips through your hands. Long hours, failures, and mundane tasks can wear you out. Here's how to keep your excitement in check:

Reconnect With Your "Why": Revisit regularly the reason you began your business. Take a minute to think about what impact you want to have and what you want to accomplish.

Take Note of Small Wins: Reward yourself for progress, however small. Each milestone is a step toward your vision.

Set Realistic Goals: Take larger tasks and divide them into smaller goals. Completing these builds momentum and requires your engagement.

Don't Have All Your Tasks in One Basket: Fight monotony. Stagger creative and administrative work to build flow.

Find Influences: Be around people that get you, read books, receive content that inspires and moves you. Connect with other entrepreneurs.

Passion, being a fire, needs fuel to continue burning. This will help you remain excited, motivated and aligned with your focus.

Avoiding Burnout

Passion is strong but can cause overworking if you're not careful. Burnout occurs when you overexert yourself for an extended period of time, resulting in fatigue and decreased motivation. To avoid burnout:

Set Boundaries: Establish and maintain clear boundaries between work and personal time. Structure regular breaks into your day and respect them.

Stay Healthy: Ensure your health, both mentally and physically. Make sure you eat well, stay active, and get enough sleep to keep your energy reserves up.

Delegate Tasks: You can't do it all yourself. Create a team or delegate draining tasks.

Take Breaks: Get away from the business from time to time to relax. Rest is not an indulgence, but a necessity.

Say No: One of the best things you can do so you're not overcommitted is to only say yes to things that are in alignment with your goals and values.

By leading effectively, you won't have to sacrifice your passion for your wellbeing.

Finding the Motivation to Keep Going When It's Tough

There isn't an entrepreneur in the world who can say that they haven't faced challenges—financial troubles, slow growth or unforeseen setbacks. In these times, it could seem challenging to stay motivated. Here are some strategies for pushing through:

Keep Things in Perspective: Understand that the struggle is temporary. Focus on your macro dream and have faith in the process.

Reach Out: Ask friends, family, or mentors for supportive encouragement. Speaking about your struggles can help you see the light more clearly.

Make mistakes: Each failure is a lesson and moves you closer to success.

Break It Down: Take things one step at a time. Breaking them down helps them feel less intense.

Celebrate Resilience: Bounce back stronger; acknowledge your will. Think of how many challenges you've already faced.

Bad times challenge your passion but also harden you. Focusing on the situation at hand helps you keep the peace through uncertainty.

I am also driven by my passion for the work in my publishing company.

I started my publishing business out of a desire to help authors and a love for storytelling. I loved everything about the whole process, from brainstorming ideas to releasing finished books. But there were times when the workload was heavy and I was really feeling the burn.

Let me start with one of my hardest challenges: having deadlines while juggling a corporate job. To keep myself motivated, I concentrated on the work I was doing — helping writers get their stories into the world. I also learned to share the load and delegate work — like new cover designs and editing.

I developed routines over time that kept me energized — such as scheduling specific hours for creative work and frequent breaks. My passion fueled me through it all, even on my challenging days. But today, I look back and see that all those challenges made me a stronger entrepreneur.

Turning Passion Into Profit

While passion is great, it's not enough to develop your business into one that is making money — you need a plan. Here's how:

Know Your Audience: Research your target customers and their needs. Customize your products or services to address their challenges.

Monetize Your Skills: Identify ways to bundle your newfound passion in ways for which people will pay money, whether they are physical goods, digital downloads or one-on-one services.

Use Technology: Use online platforms to expand your audience. Grow your business with social media, email marketing and e-commerce sites.

Monitor Your Finances: Be aware of your income and expenses. Successful financial management is key. We all want our business to be profitable.

Adapt: Listen to feedback and adjust accordingly.

Building a successful business around the things you love is fulfilling; it takes concentration, hard work, and dedication to provide value.

Finding Joy in the Journey

The destination of building a business is important but the journey is equally important. And when the work lines up with your passion, everything is meaningful. Revel in the little victories, illuminate the hard ones, and stick to what you love.

This is what gives life to your business. It's what keeps you inspired, connects you with your audience, and makes you want to build something great. If you love what you do, you will be successful.

> Pursuing passion over paychecks is less about financial prosperity and more about building the kind of life you want to live.

Conclusion: Love It or Leave It

Pursuing passion over paychecks is less about financial prosperity and more about building the kind of life you want to live. Align your business with things you love and stay excited about what you do and how you do it, and you should be able to withstand the storms that your business will face along the way.

If you have no passion for your work, people will notice. So ask yourself: Do you love what you do? If so, keep reading. If not, then it's time to find a new direction that inspires you. Life is too short to put up with anything that does not illuminate you.

CHAPTER 7
Promote Your Business, Not Your Job

When building a business while holding a full-time job, good promotion is essential to reaching your ideal audience and growing your brand. Advertisements and expensive campaigns aren't the only way to promote your business. By adopting the right strategies, you can maintain professionalism at work, utilize social media, and implement affordable tactics that will help make people aware of your business. In this chapter we're going to cover what you can do to promote your business that won't damage your relationships in your personal or professional life.

It's important to promote your business. Promotion helps you attract customers, develop trust, and expand your brand. The best product or service cannot stand out at all without continuous marketing.

Examples of why promoting your business is required:

> ➤ People who need you know you exist.

> ➤ You establish authority in your field.
> ➤ You generate a consistent stream of leads and sales.

The silver lining is there are plenty of tools and techniques that you can utilize without emptying your wallet.

Leveraging Social Media

Social media is one of the most powerful tools if you want to sell your business. It's free to use, it gives access to a wider audience, and you can directly connect with actual customers. Here's how you can make the most of it:

Choose the Right Platforms: Focus your attention on the platforms your target audience uses the most.

For example:

- Use Instagram when the business is reliant on visuals (e.g., fashion, food, art, etc.).

- Use LinkedIn for business-to-business services or networking.

- Use Facebook for community interaction or local business gatherings.

Provide Value: Offer content that educates, entertains or solves problems for your audience. Examples include:

- Give advice that relates to your industry or area of expertise.
- Behind-the-scene looks at your business.

- Testimonials or success stories from your customers.

Be Active: Comment, reply and mention to create connections. Engagement is a trust-building activity that fosters loyalty.

Schedule Posts: Plan and schedule posts ahead of time using tools like Buffer, Hootsuite, or Later. This provides timesaving and consistency.

Include Hashtags: Hashtags can help extend your reach. For example, a health coach could use the tags #WellnessTips or #HealthyLiving.

It gives you the opportunity to create a community around your brand and convert followers into paying customers and advocates for your brand.

How to Network to Build Your Business

Networking is also a very useful tool for marketing your business. Networking with the right individuals can lead to opportunities, referrals, and collaborations. Here's how to better network:

Keep Attending Events: Join industry-leading conferences, workshops or nearby meetups to engage with potential customers or partners.

This is done by joining online communities such as Facebook groups, LinkedIn groups, or forums related to your industry. Answer questions and share insights — add value!

Forget the Business Approach: Relationships should be authentic. Be a listener, be willing to help, and let your expertise come naturally.

Utilize Your Existing Network: Spread the word to friends, family, and **trusted coworkers** about your business. They may become customers or refer their friends to you!

Synergize: Form partnerships or alliances with companies. For instance, a web developer might team up with a graphic designer.

Networking involves creating connections and visibility within your field. The connections you make can help create lasting prosperity.

Finding a Balance between Personal Branding and Professionalism

If you are working full-time, it is important to find the right balance between your personal brand and professionalism when running your business. You want to scale your business but maintain your integrity at work.

Here's how to keep that balance:

Separation of Work and Business: Do not talk about your business at work, and do not use the company resources for your personal tasks.

Personal Social Media Accounts: Be certain your personal social media profiles reflect your professional reputation. Refrain from controversial posts that might tarnish your credibility.

Set Boundaries: Have separate accounts for personal and business activities. For example: Create a dedicated Instagram page for your business.

Be Valuable: Share your expertise in a way to both promote your company and cultivate your professional brand. For instance, provide industry news or tips that demonstrate your expertise.

Keeping personal branding and professional endeavors separate will allow you to maintain your integrity while nurturing your business.

Free or Low-Cost Marketing Techniques

With a little creativity, you can work with a limited budget. Below are a few low-cost ways you can start:

- **Word of Mouth:** Persuade happy customers to recommend your business to others. Provide rewards such as discounts or complimentary products for referrals.

- **Email Marketing:** Create an email list and send out regular newsletters featuring updates, offers, or helpful tips. Mailchimp and Convert Kit have free plans.

- **Content Marketing:** Start a blog or a YouTube channel and provide useful content. For example:

  o A fitness coach could upload workout videos.

  o A freelancer might offer advice on enhancing productivity.

- **Social Proof:** Show testimonials, reviews or case studies. When potential customers see others' positive experiences, they're more likely to buy.

- **SEO Optimization:** Optimize your website with keywords to improve your position in search engine results. Use free tools such as Google Keyword Planner.

- **DIY Design:** For graphics to be used in marketing materials or social media, use free tools like Canva to create non-traditional graphics.

- **Get Involved Locally:** Promote your business in person by taking part in local events, workshops, or fairs.

If you have limited resources, try the above techniques, as these strategies are cost-effective and useful.

My Publishing Business in the Spotlight: Personal Reflections

When I launched my own publishing company, I relied heavily on low-cost strategies and referrals to promote my business. It was a game-changer. By presenting behind-the-scenes content, tips for new authors and testimonials from satisfied clients, I amassed a loyal following.

Networking also proved vital. Networking at book fairs and hosting writing groups also led me to prospective clients and collaborators. One benefit that I gained from this is a regular stream of referrals, which helped my business a lot.

It also was important to balance personal branding and professionalism. There were dedicated social media accounts for my business and my personal profiles remained professional. This approach helped me grow my brand without crossing professional lines in my full-time job.

Consistency is Key

Promotion is not a one-off—it is a continuous effort. Develop a marketing calendar and follow it. Posting three times a week on social media, sending monthly newsletters, attending one event per quarter — all of these regular efforts create momentum and visibility.

Here's how to stay consistent:

Set realistic goals: Pursue marketing campaigns that work with your time and perception.

Measure Results: Use tools such as Google Analytics or social media analytics to track the performance of your initiatives.

Fine-tune: Test various techniques and modify your approach to align with what is most effective.

You can build trust and strong presence in your industry through consistency.

Your Business, Your Brand: In Closing

When it comes to marketing your business, it's more than just getting customers—it's about creating a brand that embodies your values and resonates with your audience. You can grow your business while keeping a professional image by utilizing social media, networking effectively and utilizing low-cost marketing methods.

And you don't have to have a big budget or a fancy campaign to do so. Concentrate on this: Provide value, build relationships, and be consistent. Your business will flourish with diligence and hard work.

Your brand is a reflection of who you are. Do it authentically, and the right audience will recognize you.

Remember – promote your business, not your job.

CHAPTER 8
Stack Skills: Leverage Your 9-to-5 Into an Asset

A paycheck isn't necessarily the only thing your day job can offer; it can also be an excellent breeding ground for the skills you'll need to become an entrepreneur. Many of the things you do at work can transfer to running your business and save you time, money and effort. In this chapter, you will learn how to identify transferable skills from your job that can be leveraged for your business.

What is Skill Stacking?

The concept of skill stacking is simply merging different skills together to gain a unique advantage. This isn't so much about being a master of everything but developing a variety of competencies that work together. Your full-time job exposes you to numerous skills that can help you grow your business.

For example:

- Someone who teaches can use those lesson-planning skills to create online courses or workshops.

- An IT guy can leverage their technical skills to create efficient systems for their company.

By applying what you already know in unique ways, you can have a competitive advantage in entrepreneurship through skill stacking.

Leveraging Skills Developed on the Job

Your current job, a previous one or even one you can do in the future most likely have the direct or indirect skills that would benefit your business.

Let's look at workplace skills and how they can lead to success in the entrepreneurship field:

Project Management:

Work Experience: Managing deadlines, coordinating resources, and ensuring tasks are completed in a timely manner.

Business Application: Coordinating product launches, planning marketing campaigns, and managing client projects.

Communication:

Work Experience: Framing emails, pitching ideas, or engaging co-workers.

Business Application: Writing convincing messages to customers, negotiating with suppliers, and building relationships with partners

Problem-Solving:

Work Experience: Innovation or improvement of processes or solutions to problems.

Business Application: Managing customer issues, improving workflows, and rectifying business hurdles.

Budgeting and Financial Management:

Work Experience: Monitoring departmental budgets or overseeing expenditures.

Business Application: Financial planning and monitoring, investment planning

Leadership:

Work Experience: You can be a team lead or help your colleagues from day to day.

Business Application: Forming and leading your team.

Time Management:

Work Experience: Prioritizing tasks to deadlines.

Business Application: Stay ahead on business by balancing responsibilities.

These are just a few ways in which your job can arm you with the tools for success as an entrepreneur.

Transferable Skills

Here are examples of transferable skills in action, and examples of how you could apply them to different business contexts:

Marketing Expertise:

A corporate marketer may use their expertise with branding and social media to boost sales for their side hustle making custom jewelry. They use their talent to produce flashy advertisements and establish a vibrant online presence.

Customer Service:

A Help Desk Operator would use their skills answering customer questions to provide service for their online site. Their skills in customer service allow them to promptly resolve problems, which makes for loyal customers.

Technical Skills:

An IT professional develops a website for his business using his programming skills and saves thousands of dollars on web development.

Event Planning:

An administrative assistant who organizes corporate events uses those same organizational abilities to successfully host workshops and networking events for their business.

These examples illustrate how skills you already possess can help you to build your business.

Finding a Training Room in Your Day Job

Do not look at your job as something hindering you from becoming an entrepreneur; think of it as one big learning opportunity. Every task, project or challenge is an opportunity to build and hone skills that can serve your business. Here's how to do your job with this mindset:

Spot the Gaps: Determine in what sectors you can acquire new skills or improve your existing ones. As an example, volunteer for projects involving leadership, technology or creative problem-solving.

Seize Learning Opportunities: Go beyond your day job. This may include going to training, shadowing colleagues, or soliciting feedback from managers.

Observe and Adapt: Be aware of how your organization runs. What are the systems, tools, or strategies they use? Customize these practices to fit your particular business needs.

Ask Questions: Work with colleagues or mentors who know more about these topics than you do. Their wisdom may contribute to you becoming a business guru.

As you treat your day job as proving ground, you'll have your work experience and the confidence to apply these skills to your business.

Bringing Together Different Skills for Greater Impact

Skill stacking is more than just having skills, though — it's also about the way you combine them to create something unique. For example:

- Even a writer with basic graphic design skills can create great looking content to draw in more visitors to their blog.

- A coding enthusiast can start learning the sales pitch of an e-commerce platform.

- If a photographer is great at social media marketing, they can find more clients and build their brand.

Consider the overlap in your skillsets and how you can combine them to offer your business unique insight or solutions.

Having a Job and a Business at the Same Time

Take advantage of your day job as a learning opportunity but be careful not to overload yourself. Here are some tips to help both these areas flourish:

Set Limits: Even at home, separate work and business activities. During your personal time, have your business in mind, but be cautious of any conflict of interest.

Set Realistic Expectations: Do not set unrealistic expectations for yourself in either area. You also need to set reasonable targets for your business; do not disappoint your employer.

Use Downtime Wisely: During work breaks or slow workdays, jot down ideas, notes, or figure out business actions (if allowed).

Celebrate Progress: Value what skills you are developing at your job, and how they are paving your entrepreneurial journey.

Balancing these responsibilities can be challenging; however, the benefits outweigh the efforts.

MY SKILL STACK

I'll share a little about my skill stacking experience.

When I first started my business, I relied a lot on skills I had in my full-time job. For example:

Skills from workplace presentations carried over into persuasive pitches for clients and speaking from the stage.

When my agency brought motivational speakers in, I paid close attention to their methods and delivery. I applied what I thought they executed well to enhance my external speaking gigs for my business.

The budgeting know-how learned managing departmental expenses became invaluable when trying to map out my business finances.

Seeing my job as a training ground reframed how I looked at it. Instead of seeing my role as limiting, I found it an opportunity to learn about something different and grow in a new way. This mentality laid the groundwork for building confidence and was ultimately foundational in building my business.

Exercises to Practice Your Skills

Here are some exercises for helping you recognize and amplify transferable skills:

Skill inventory: Create a list of skills that you use in your job. Next to each, note how it could be relevant to your business.

Gap Analysis: Skills your business requires but you have not developed. Seek opportunities to develop those skills at work.

Skill Challenge: Pick a skill to level up monthly. For instance, work on public speaking, or use a new software tool.

Feedback Sessions: Seek feedback from peers or supervisors on your strengths and areas for development. You will use their feedback to inform your development.

These practices help you proactively stack your skills.

The bottom line: Your job is your asset.

How Skill Stacking Changed My Life

Before I discovered the power of skill stacking, I felt stuck and unfulfilled in my job. I dreamed of running my own business but as a single parent with two young children, taking that leap felt irresponsible. My job required little of me, leaving me watching the clock and feeling imprisoned by the monotony.

Then I came across the book *Caught Between a Job and a Dream*, and it changed everything. The idea of using my job as a resource sparked a shift in my mindset. I began viewing my workplace as a training ground instead of a trap. I signed up for professional development opportunities—public speaking, time management, mentoring—and attended every seminar I could. While others saw these as chances to escape their desks, I absorbed every detail, from the speakers' tone and cadence to their delivery.

This shift in perspective reignited my passion for work. I was getting paid to build skills that would serve both my job and my dreams. Over the years, I've applied everything I learned to grow my businesses, from running a female mentoring organization for 13 years to building a successful coaching practice and now managing my publishing enterprise.

The core principle remains timeless: Leverage your current situation to prepare for the next level. My journey proves that the job you have today can be a steppingstone to the future you envision.

Take this as your light bulb moment. Reframe how you see your job. Make it work for you by identifying opportunities to learn, grow, and stack skills.

> Your current job is not just a source of income; it's the path to your future entrepreneurial success.

Ready to stack your skills? Your future self will thank you.

Your current job is not just a source of income; it's the path to your future entrepreneurial success. So by stacking skills, and by leveraging what you learn at work, you'll create a powerful foundation for your business. Use each task, challenge, and project as a snapshot of how to improve, and take those lessons to create a thriving business.

Skill stacking isn't about being perfect — it's about being better. The more you mix and polish your skills, the more unique and dynamic your business will be. Transform your job into an asset and then unleash the entrepreneurial beast within.

CHAPTER 9
Fund Your Freedom: Use Your Job to Support Your Dream

The first and most significant advantage of starting your business while still maintaining your 9-to-5 is the financial security it gives you. Your paycheck can serve you as a superpower for funding your early-stage entrepreneurial journey, allowing you to avoid risk of debt. This chapter covers how to budget, save, reinvest and keep separate business and personal finances for the long run!

Let me say this up front: Don't let anyone make you feel like you are less of an entrepreneur because you maintain a full-time job while pursuing your dream. Over the years I've heard people insinuate that if you have a job, you are not a real entrepreneur. It's almost like full-time entrepreneurs look down on those who are pursuing their dreams while also working. That's nonsense. In fact, people who are balancing both are the real MVPs if you ask me. Managing to hit 6 figures in my business while still working my 9-to-5—that was the real flex. However, I do acknowledge that taking the risk of stepping out there to become a full-time entrepreneur could probably move you to six or seven figures faster because you would be dedicating your efforts full-time to your business. It took me 4 years to hit 6 figures, but it happened almost effortlessly. In fact, I didn't even realize it had happened until my business coach asked me to run my end of year numbers. It was exciting. I thought to myself, *Wow, if I hit 6 figures this easily while working my full-time job, how much more could I generate if I was a full-time entrepreneur pouring all my time and effort into my business?*

You are the only one who can assess whether or not taking the risk is right for you and your family. To be honest, of the female entrepreneurs I've followed over the years who have proudly and loudly bragged about the fact that they quit their 9-to-5 to become full time entrepreneurs, probably 98% of them have had husbands backing them. They have dipped into their 401Ks, depleted savings accounts, and maybe even borrowed from family and friends to stay afloat. Many who jump out there without a solid plan tend to revert back to a 9-to-5 within the first year or two. Remember, social media is only the highlight reel. You never know what is going on behind the scenes. I think any way you choose to pursue your dream is admirable.

Now, let's dive into why your day job is the key to your entrepreneurial success.

Launching a business typically involves some initial costs, whether it's having a website built or buying inventory. Unlike a loan or an outside investor, your job can serve as a funder. Here's why:

Stable Income: Your salary supports your livelihood and the growth of your business.

Risk Reduction: A job is an excellent way to lower financial pressure so that you can take calculated risks for your business.

Turning your job into a fire for your dream allows you to build your business without financial pressure.

How to Prepare a Budget for Your Business

You need to have a good budget that forms the base of financial progress. It enables you to allocate resources smartly and monitor your journey. To create a business budget that works for you, follow these steps:

Evaluate Your Income – Evaluate your after-tax monthly income. It will help you understand how much you can invest.

Log Expenses: Write down all of your personal expenses, from rent to utilities and groceries to debt payments. From this figure, subtract those payments to see how much you can save or invest.

Set priorities: Determine your business's most urgent needs, such as equipment, marketing or software subscriptions. Work top-down on issues with highest priority.

Pay Yourself: Determine how much of your paycheck goes into the business. For instance, perhaps you keep 20% for business expenses and put away 10% for an emergency fund.

Check In Regularly: Go over your budget every month to make sure you're on track and adjust as necessary.

By having a solid budget, you will stay on top of your finances without losing sight of your goals.

Saving for Your Business

Saving money is the cornerstone of any healthy financial life. Here are a few tips and strategies for saving:

Automate Your Savings: If you start automatically transferring money to an account specifically for your business, it becomes easier to save without needing to think about it each month. This helps maintain consistency and diminishes the urge to shop.

Minimize Unneeded Spending: Examine your spending habits and cut out unnecessary spending, such as going out to eat or subscription services you do not use.

Use Sudden Wealth Wisely: Redirect bonuses, tax refunds or any surprise income directly into your business savings rather than spending it mindlessly.

Create a Savings Habit: By saving even a small amount regularly, you will learn how to accumulate money over time. The difference: For example, $50 a week grows to $2,600 in a year.

When you save regularly, there is a financial cushion, allowing you the freedom to invest back into your business.

Reinvesting for Growth

Substantial reinvestment is an essential aspect of any growing business. Similar to a business, do not take all of your earnings out; actually put them back in for future growth. Here's how:

- **Focus on High Impact Areas:** Invest in activities that will drive the most growth: marketing, product development, technology upgrades, etc.

- **Set Goals:** Establish clear reinvestment objectives, like launching a new product or broadening your customer base.

- **Scale Gradually:** Begin with minimal investment and re-invest as your company earns money.

Reinvestment allows your business to grow and adapt while also remaining competitive and scalable. Also, for each reinvestment, track return on investment.

Managing Financial Risks

As with every business, when it comes to entrepreneurship there is business risk, but how you manage that risk ultimately determines the stability of your finances. Here are some tips to reduce risks:

- **Create an Emergency Savings Account:** Set aside three to six months of living expenses to prepare for the unexpected.

- **Go Lean:** Don't overspend in the beginning. Cut out what you need to and refrain from frivolous spending.

- **Validate Demand:** In the early stages, avoid committing to large production runs, and instead invest in smaller tests to measure interest and demand for your offers.

- **Get Insurance:** Look into business insurance to cover liabilities, property damage, or other risks.

What you do in the early stages of your business will allow you to manage risks to be in control of everything.

Separation of Personal and Business Expenses

Separating your personal and business finances is essential for clear, organized, and legally compliant finances. Here's how to do so effectively:

- **Open a Separate Business Account:** Use a separate account for all business-related deposits and withdrawals. This helps tracking expenses and income much easier.

- **Get Different Credit Cards:** Open up a business credit card to ensure that purchases made for business are separate from personal spending.

- **Monitor Expenses:** Keep records of all business expenditures with relevant evidence such as receipts and invoices. This makes tax preparation and financial analysis cost-effective and easier.

- **Pay Yourself a Salary:** To avoid being inconsistent with your finances, use a fixed rate from your business profit instead of dipping into funds.

- **Seek Professional Help:** Hire an accountant or financial advisor to help you organize your financial records in line with tax regulations.

Separating your finances protects your personal assets and gives you a clear view of your business's financial health.

Long-Term Financial Success Tips

Reaching financial freedom does not happen overnight; it takes time, energy, and resourcefulness. Below are some more tips for long-term success:

- **Set Financial Goals:** Define short- and long-term financial objectives for your business. For example, in a year, save $10,000 to get your business to a new level or expansion.

- **Observe Your Cash Flow:** Keep track of the money coming in and going out in your business. This can help you stay on top of your finances.

- **Manage Debt Wisely:** Be selective about the credit you use and pay off high-interest debts as quickly as possible.

- **Keep Things in Balance:** These are some of the most rewarding investments you can make!

- **Celebrate the Small Wins:** Acknowledge your successes and treat yourself for hitting financial milestones.

These are the habits that will help you create a long-lasting and lucrative business over the years.

Personal Insights: I started my publishing business with my own money.

Establishing my publishing business while working my full-time day job allowed me to pay the bills in advance while waiting for royalties. I set aside money from each paycheck to pay for things like website development, software subscriptions, and marketing materials. Setting solid priorities, and sticking to my budget, I avoided unnecessary debt.

If you ask me, one of the most important things I learned was the necessity of reinvesting. I invested profits in improving my services, hiring freelancers, and expanding my reach rather than spending them right away. It helped my business to grow over the years and kept my finances in check.

Keeping personal and business finances separate was also a game changer. Separate accounts made bookkeeping easier and gave me a good view of my business's financial health.

The Freedom Associated with Financial Discipline

It takes discipline and patience to fund your business through your job, but the rewards are worth it. Financial freedom enables you to chase your goals. By using a sensible budget, holding on to your earnings and reinvesting for growth, you'll be establishing a firm groundwork for long-term success.

Your job is more than just a means of making a living; it's a means of lighting your dream. Use it wisely, and you'll make great strides toward living the life you dream of.

Conclusion: Transform Your Job into Your Launching Platform

Your 9-to-5 job is relative to your ability to chase your entrepreneurial goal as much as it is a way to pay the bills. You can build a business that runs as a successful entity, and in doing so, you aren't gambling your financial position away by leveraging your income, taking on risks and separating finances.

Keep your eye on the prize, your head in the game, and don't be wasteful with your resources. The right job can be your ticket to the freedom and the success you're striving for.

CHAPTER 10
Invest Like a Boss: Stop Being Cheap with Your Vision

Making a successful business takes time and work—and just as many, if not more, smart investments. Investing in the right tools, professional education, and/or resources can make all the difference. This chapter will explain why you should focus on long-term growth, share some real-life examples of powerful investments, and encourage you to stop skimping on your vision.

Why Investing Matters

Any business is only as solid as its foundation. Overlooking key tools or skipping necessary expense can save money today while hampering your growth and costing you more long term. Choosing good resources is an investment that guarantees:

- **Reduced stress:** The right tools free up time and energy for what's really important.

- **Credibility:** Quality products, service, and branding help enhance customer trust.

- **Sustainability:** The right investments enable you to build a scalable and lasting company.

- **Continued Education:** Additional training ensures you stay updated on industry trends and enhance your skillset.

Investing in your business isn't just an expense – it's a promise to your success.

Areas to Invest In

Some critical areas where strategic investments can bring rewarding payoffs include:

- **Tools and Tech**: Investing in trustworthy tools streamlines operations on a daily basis. Examples include:

  - **Project management software**: Tools like Trello or Asana help keep tasks in order and deadlines met.

  - **Accounting Software**: QuickBooks, FreshBooks, or One Minute Bookkeeper make bookkeeping and financial management more straightforward.

  - **Design Tools:** Use tools like Canva and Adobe Creative Suite to create professional marketing materials.

- **Education and Training:** You want to stay competitive and learn about how to make your business better. Consider Udemy or Coursera online courses.

- **Relevant workshops or certification programs.**

- **Mentorship programs or guided development from seasoned entrepreneurs.**

- **Marketing and Branding:** Your brand is a representation of your business. Having professionals design your website and advertise your products definitely increases your visibility and credibility.

- **Talent:** Hiring the right Freelancers, consultants, and team members will accelerate your business growth. Try to narrow down the types of positions to those that will fill your needs, such as graphic designers, virtual assistants, or social media managers.

- **Infrastructure:** If you need a website, office space, or manufacturing equipment, make sure you have it and that it's the right fit to grow.

Investing strategically in these areas gets you better results, more customers, and faster goal achievement.

Real Life Examples: Investments That Yielded Returns

When I founded my publishing business, I soon learned that cutting corners wasn't going to take me very far. Here are a few investments I made that contributed to my growth in one way or another:

Professional Book Covers: Not wanting to skimp on quality, I employed a graphic designer. Though I could have used free tools, the professional touch helped me and my clients stand out and brought in more clients.

Email Marketing Platform: Investing in a paid email marketing service like Mailchimp (which has a free version) allowed me to send personalized campaigns, track engagement, and grow my audience. This translated into increased revenue and more robust customer relationships.

Website Development: Invested money in developing a professional website with easy navigation and an attractive design. This initial investment pays off, as it adds credibility and enhances user engagement.

Educational Courses: I took courses in marketing and business management, in which I learned strategies I still use today. These lessons paid off tenfold in the way I approached my decision-making and efficiency.

All of these investments added value to my business and proved that smart spending is necessary.

How to Decide Where to Invest

Not all expenses are worth making, so invest wisely. Here's how to find the best places for your business:

Evaluate Your Needs: Look for challenges or hurdles that you have in your operations. So, for example, if managing tasks is too much for you, a project management tool could be your next investment.

Stress the High-Impact Areas: Concentrate on areas that will return on investment considerably, such as customer experience improvement or increased efficiency.

Explore Alternatives: Research tools, services, and courses to find the right fit for you. Seek reviews, referrals or free trials.

Start Small: Invest in inexpensive solutions before venturing into larger expenditures. For instance, begin with a simple form of a software tool and upgrade when required.

Set a Budget: Allocate some of your revenue to reinvest. This keeps you within a budget for essential costs without overstretching your finances.

Good decision-making makes sure you get the maximum out of your investment, while minimizing any unnecessary cost.

Adopting a Long-Term Vision

Entrepreneurship is not about quick wins — it's about sustainability. It prevents you from being reactive and short-sighted. Here's what you can do to adopt this way of thinking:

Plan for the Long Game: How will your investments serve your business a year, five years or a decade from now?

Develop Scalable Systems: Implement tools and processes that can scale with your business. For example, select a customer relationship management (CRM) solution that will grow alongside an expanding customer base.

Be patient: Certain investments are long term and take a while to yield results. Keep doing your work, and believe in yourself.

Actualize Growth: It's important to revisit your goals and revise investments as your needs change.

Taking a long-term perspective on every decision ensures lasting success with every decision you make.

A Guide to Overcoming Spending Anxiety

I know it can feel scary to spend money, especially when you're starting out in your business. But neglecting your investments can trap you. Here's how to conquer this fear:

- **Change Your Mindset:** Treat investments as opportunities, not costs. Every dollar well spent puts you closer to your goals.

- **Start With Small Things:** Start by investing in small things and you can increase them slowly as your business grows.

- **Track Results:** Measure the effect of your investments on your business. Making small step-by-step changes will help you build confidence when you see measurable differences.

Risk taking is an essential element of entrepreneurship. Trust yourself to make choices that help your business move forward.

- **Follow the Right Path:** Look at successful entrepreneurs and what money and time they invested. Their stories may inspire and reassure you.

Risk taking is an essential element of entrepreneurship. Trust yourself to make choices that help your business move forward.

Common Mistakes to Avoid

Investing in your business is important, but equally important is avoiding common mistakes:

Overcapacity Early: Getting started and spending well before you make money can be a drain on your bank account. Begin small and expand as you develop.

Not Caring about Quality: Low-priced solutions may save you some money at the start, but they can also yield poor results and later cost more in the long run.

Negligent Investing: Investing without sufficient research can lead to a waste of resources. Consider options before making a commitment.

Ignoring Non-essential Expenses: From your budget, focus only on essentials in the context of your tools or services, whatever is more directly tied to your operations or customers.

Not Reassessing: Regularly reassess your investments to see if they're still working for you. Ditch any tools or subscriptions that no longer serve you.

Steering clear of these mistakes will allow you to make better, more impactful investment choices.

WHAT I LEARNED:

Invest in Your Vision

Your business is a manifestation of your vision, and the vision needs the best. But investing in quality tools, education, and resources represents an investment in your success. It's not about spending wildly—it's about investing in strategies that contribute toward growth and sustainability.

Quit being stingy with your vision. Instead, take a long-term view, target the highest-impact areas, and believe that the right investments will yield results. Your future self (and your business) will thank you.

RECAP:
Creating Your Road to Six Figures

Well done for making it to the last chapter of this book! You've learned to create a six-figure business while working a 9-to-5. From actionable strategies to mindset shifts and practical tools, each chapter has been designed to empower you in the pursuit of your entrepreneurial dreams. In this final chapter, we will summarize the key takeaways, highlight the significance of resiliency and self-belief, and urge you to implement the insights into your own life, starting today.

Key Lessons from the Book

We covered the steps needed to balance a full-time job with building a thriving business throughout this journey. Here's a rundown of the major takeaways:

Have the Right Mindset: If you help yourself, half of your work is done. The willingness to take some risks, to embrace a growth mindset and then to bet on yourself is the way to overcome and excel.

Leverage Your Job as a Resource: Your 9-to-5 gives you financial resources, skills and the actual base to fund your business. Use it as a resource, not a restriction.

Your Most Important Asset Is Time: You know how and when to take paid leave, when to take the weekend, and even when to take two weeks off and do nothing. This is where planning and prioritization come into play.

Develop a Support Network: Assigning tasks and forming a requisite team enables your business to thrive without your direct involvement.

Systems Make It Easy: From automating through systems to streamlined processes that free your time and make your business operations consistent.

You Are Motivated by Passion: Establishing a business that aligns with your passions enables long-lasting motivation and success in the long-term.

Market with Intention: Add efforts on social networking, organic visibility, and budget-friendly marketing strategies that help connect you with your ideal customers.

Stack Your Skills: Use the skills you learn at your job to come up with creative business solutions that others might not think of.

Invest While It's Safe: Any expenditure, whether on tools, education, or anything else, strengthens your base for the same.

These lessons build upon each other, providing a guide for your success.

Resilience, strategy, and self-belief go a long way. But one thing to note is that entrepreneurship is full of ups and downs. It takes resilience to get through disappointments, strategy to remain on task, and self-belief to keep going. Let's dig deeper into why these traits are so essential:

Resilience: Challenges are a given, but how you react to these challenges will determine your success. Resilience means holding fast to our determination, learning from our missteps, and adjusting to the changing tides.

For example: When sales decline or challenges appear, resilient entrepreneurs change their approach rather than quit.

Action Step: Treat each failure as an opportunity to learn. Assess what has been difficult, and what lessons to take forward.

Strategy: An effective strategy helps to keep you focused and avoids wasting time and effort. Strategy empowers you to work on the right things at the right time.

For example, focus on high-impact activities — such as marketing and customer engagement — instead of spreading yourself too thin.

Action Step: Write out a plan for the week with things you want to accomplish or tasks you want to get done. Dive into your progress regularly and see if it's going in the right direction.

Believe in Yourself: Confidence in your ability to create keeps you going. When you have confidence in yourself, you are more inclined to take risks and go after opportunities.

For example, entrepreneurs who believe in their vision tend to pitch it more often, recruit customers, and innovate.

Action Step: Acknowledge and celebrate every achievement, even the small ones, to nurture your confidence.

Entrepreneur Journey refers to the journey from struggling to achieve your dream to making it all happen. Develop these traits to keep your drive alive and stay on track with your ambitions.

Action Step: Start today.

You can read this book and find it engaging, but if you do not implement its insights, the information is useless. One step at a time—just begin. Here's how to get started on building your six-figure business:

Define Your Vision:

List out your goals for the next year, five years, and forever.

Determine what success will look like and what you need to start doing in order to make that happen.

Start Small:

Take one step toward the beginning — building your website, designing a product, or even setting up a social media page.

Develop a mindset of progress, not perfection.

Set a Schedule:

Set aside dedicated time blocks for your business, even if it's just a couple of hours a week.

Consider this time non-negotiable and follow through.

Track Your Finances:

Research ways to budget for your business and begin saving for initial expenses.

Another tip: Separate personal and business finances to stay organized and prepared for growth.

Stay Accountable:

Share your goals with someone you trust — a friend, mentor or community. Be accountable — this makes you focused and committed.

When you start today, it creates forward momentum and turns dreams into reality.

The Importance of Consistency

Consistency is what it takes to become successful. Small, consistent actions over time lead to big change. Whether it's writing for social media, saving for your company's office space or learning something new, concentrated effort compounds into something big over time.

Here's how to remain consistent:

Habit: Establish daily or weekly rituals to support your goals. For example, Monday evening work for marketing or Sunday afternoon for planning your week.

Remove Distractions: Take out everything that is costing you time from your business.

Savor your progress: Embrace your accomplishments, even the small ones. Every step forward is a win.

Consistent action helps to build trust with your audience, develops your business, and keeps you moving forward toward success.

Your Six-Figure Vision

Now imagine where you are going to be a year, five years, and ten years from now, thanks to the steps you take after reading this book. Imagine that you are becoming a successful business owner, gaining financial independence as well as participating in living a life with purpose and freedom.

Your six-figure vision isn't just a number on a bank balance — it's about building a business that reflects your values, your passions, and the lifestyle you want. This vision is completely within your grasp with the right mindset, strategy, and action.

As you start this journey, keep in mind:

You Are Enough: You already have everything you need within yourself to succeed. Believe in yourself and don't stop learning.

All Challenges Are Steps: Every challenge is an opportunity in disguise to become stronger and wiser.

It Takes Time: Patience and persistence. Rewards will show up through consistent effort.

The journey to six figures isn't always an easy one, but it's worth it. Stay focused, stay strong, and believe in yourself.

Conclusion: Your Road Toward Success

This book has handed you the tools, the strategies, the inspiration—everything you need to make a six-figure business with a side hustle on top of your 9-to-5. The time has come to execute and make your vision become a reality. Remember:

- A firm plan, along with the bravery to move forward, is the only path to success.

- Rely on resilience, strategies, and self-belief to get you through challenges!

- Small things do add up in a big way over time.

Your journey begins now. So no matter if you're just getting started, honing in on your goals, or expanding your business, each and every one of those steps take you one step closer to your dreams. The life you dream of awaits you; go out and make it.

To your success,

Kimmoly

www.ingramcontent.com/pod-product-compliance
Lightning Source LLC
Chambersburg PA
CBHW041428200328
41914CB00009B/1219